TO LINDA,

BEST @ 15 AEST

[Portobello Cookbook]

Porto
cook

40 QUICK AND EASY RECIPES

ILLUSTRATIONS BY ALEXANDRA MALDONADO

b e l l o
b o o k

Jack Czarnecki

ARTISAN   NEW YORK

To my mother, Wanda, my wife, Heidi, and my kids,
Sonja, Christopher, and Stefan

Editor: Ann ffolliott
Production director: Hope Koturo

Published in 1997 by ARTISAN
a division of Workman Publishing Company, Inc.
708 Broadway
New York, NY 10003-9555

Library of Congress Cataloging-in-Publication Data
Czarnecki, Jack.
Portobello cookbook / Jack Czarnecki : illustrations by Alexandra Maldonado.
Includes index.
ISBN 1-885183-75-5
1. Cookery (Mushrooms) 2. Mushrooms, Edible. I. Title.
TX804.C924 1997
641.6'58—dc21   96-47967
CIP

Printed in Japan
10 9 8 7 6 5 4 3 2
Second Printing

contents

introduction

[The mushroom with the name nobody knows how to spell]

I'll be the first to admit it: I was late in appreciating this wonderful mushroom. When I wrote my first book in 1985, the portobello mushrooms I saw were ridiculously expensive and not really very nice—rather, they resembled overblown versions of supermarket mushrooms. I was so unimpressed that I didn't bother mentioning them. Then, in 1987, at a symposium on mushrooms at Kennett Square, Pennsylvania, I caught sight of the most beautiful cultivated exotic mushrooms I had ever seen. They were portobellos from Phillips Mushroom Farms in Avondale, Pennsylvania. I was so impressed with the suede leather look of the caps and the meaty fullness of the mushrooms that we have had them on the menu at our restaurant ever since.

Of course, it's interesting to speculate as to why this mushroom is booming. More than 30 million pounds of portobello mushrooms were sold in the United States last year. I believe that the size is what makes this mushroom so popular and, yes, so American. This oddball giant of the fungal world is a mushroom that you can really sink your teeth into, like Texas barbecue. It is satisfying like steak. In fact, the comment I hear most often about the portobello is that it's so much like meat. Well, it is and it isn't, but I'll get into that a little later.

This collection of recipes will get you started using portobellos. In our restaurant, we have used portobellos in many different dishes, combining them with meat, fish, and vegetables, or using them as the main feature of a dish. This book contains many of those recipes, adapted for the home cook, as well as some new ones. Most of these recipes are very simple and quick, using a minimum of ingredients and optimizing flavor. Remember, simplicity is the key to the successful use of this giant mushroom.

WHAT IS A PORTOBELLO?

A portobello mushroom is a very large cremini, and a cremini is a brown or cream-colored version of the white button mushroom *(Agaricus brunnescens,* formerly known as *A. bisporus).* It has been erroneously reported that the white button is the *A. bisporus* and the cremini the *A. brunnescens,* but they are both the same genus and species; the cremini is a brown variety. With one important distinction, the flavor of the portobello is the same as that of the common supermarket mushroom, except it is more distinct because it is older and more developed. The gills on the underside of the mushroom have progressed to a greater degree from the pale pink stage at their first break.

Most people buy white button mushrooms with the cap closed around the stem to ensure maximum freshness. But as the mushrooms develop and the gills become exposed and darken, the flavor becomes more intense. Thus older, less fresh-looking white buttons that have their dark gills exposed are, in fact, more flavorful than their closed siblings. Since portobellos, by virtue of their size, are always well opened with developed gills, they also have more flavor.

Interestingly, these giant cremini were once considered oddballs and were treated more like weeds than mushrooms. When cremini cultivation began, the first runs (or crops) would often be abnormally large. Because cremini were expected to be the same size as white buttons, these giants were shunned—and even discarded—until the next run yielded a size more acceptable to the market. Now, you may occasionally see the more "acceptable" sizes of cremini marketed as "baby portobellos," when in reality they are normal-size cremini. Don't be fooled.

In 1985, Phillips Mushroom Farms decided to market the larger first-run cremini as portobello mushrooms—the spelling of this name remains controversial; Phillips calls them "portabellas"—recognizing their potential from a culinary standpoint. The rest is history.

ABOUT THAT NAME

Nobody seems to know where the name portobello comes from. At first, when most people thought that the mushrooms were imported from Italy, it was assumed that the name was Italian. The name "portobello" stuck until somebody decided to make it even more Italian by spelling it "portabella." This spelling is the one used by most commercial growers and wholesalers these days, but "portobello" remains on menus and in vegetable markets. You can also find the variations "portabello" and "portobella."

BUYING AND KEEPING PORTOBELLO MUSHROOMS

Unlike button mushrooms or cremini, which are almost always purchased with the cap closed around the stem, portobellos are more mature and larger, so the cap is wide open, well free from the stem. This flared-out characteristic with the gills clearly visible is a major difference between portobellos and their small cousins. Do not expect to find portobellos with closed caps.

Large whole portobellos, including caps, stems, and roots, can generally be purchased only individually. Prices will be higher in specialty stores. One can frequently find a better deal in large supermarkets, where the quality is as good as that found in specialty stores, regardless of packaging. It is often the case, however, that very large portobellos (over 4 inches in diameter) command a premium price, even in supermarkets.

Retail packages of portobello mushrooms come primarily in two forms. Whole caps (2-4 caps per pack) without stems are readily available in 6-ounce packages. Perhaps the most common form of retail package is the 6-ounce group of sliced caps. These have a shelf life of about ten days and sell for the same price as the whole caps in 6-ounce packages. A third, though less common form, of portobello comes in 1- to 1 1/2-inch chunks, also in a 6-ounce retail pack. These are good for tossing in salads raw or for threading on a skewer for grilling or broiling, especially with steak.

Note also that mushrooms in general often go on special in supermarkets. Produce managers keep a wary eye on the amount of time the mushrooms have been in stock. Any sign of browning and they reduce the price, sometimes drastically. You should be able to take advantage of such specials knowing that, just because the mushrooms aren't pretty, doesn't mean that they aren't still very good for cooking.

Fresh, right-from-the-farm portobellos have a slightly shiny and mostly smooth cream or light tan colored cap of with small, scaly dark portions. They range in diameter from $2^1/2$ up to 8 inches! They tend to snap when broken, although even young mushrooms can sometimes be quite pliant. Cross-section slices of the mushroom are pearly white with some pale light brown sections, and even some yellowish sections. The gills underneath the cap are gray to light brown in the fresh specimens, and are well defined and evenly spaced with occasional wavy areas near the stem. The stem has a stuffed but not full feel, and you will occasionally even notice hollow parts within the stem, which can make them awkward to slice thin. Fresh portobellos stay in this form for four to five days, after which they undergo the changes described below. When you buy the mushrooms, bring them home and keep them refrigerated in a plastic or paper bag.

Older portobello caps become darker and develop very noticeable wrinkles. They also lose their sheen. Older specimens are also much more pliable than young ones and don't snap when broken. The cross-section slices are various shades of bruised brown and light brown, and the gills are much darker. The transformation from young and fresh to older and brown happens fairly quickly, but that does not mean the older mushrooms are inferior. Furthermore, even after the portobellos have undergone this change they remain in this state for up to three weeks, as the mushroom gills become darker and the caps more wrinkled and pliable. As they age further, the caps can become slimy, especially in those plastic packages. However, rinsing will take care of that if the mushrooms have not gone too far. Smell them to make sure they still smell earthy, not spoiled.

Now, on the subject of old versus new, there are some things you should realize. The younger mushrooms, sautéed or braised, have a much lighter color and softer, spongier texture; they are quite mild and pleasing in flavor. As the mushrooms grow older and the gills mature, these same mushrooms appear darker after sautéing or braising. They also have a chewier texture. But more important, the flavor becomes more intense. In some instances, they taste even better than young mushrooms. Older mushrooms, for example, make a superior duxelles (see page 31). Also, the older whole caps do not have to be prebaked before grilling or baking, because they have already lost some of their moisture.

Don't bother to freeze portobellos. They get really ugly when defrosted and look like oozing sponges, caused by the mushroom liquid eager to make its exit.

THE GILLS

From a cooking standpoint, the most important part of the portobello is the gills. They start out a pale pink color, then gradually turn brown, eventually turning a dark chocolate brown. As the gills become darker, the flavor becomes more intense. You must remember that those darker gills yield a darker sautéed mixture or darker sauce. Some chefs prefer to remove the gills from older mushrooms, but this is not necessary when you use very fresh portobellos. And even young portobellos will yield darker sauces than white button mushrooms. If you want a sauce that will not darken, remove the gills or use white buttons.

I like to use the gills for is a "truffle" garnish (see page 23). I scrape the gills off the underside of the cap, then sprinkle them onto a white plate. We also call these shavings "confetti."

THE STEM

Although the stem of the portobello mushroom is the least favored part, it is the firmest part of the mushroom and also has good flavor. Stems are great for duxelles, and can be sliced (fairly thickly) for use in sauté dishes, as well. Because they have interior gaps, and can even be hollow in spots, they are difficult to cut into even pieces. But they are still wonderful added to stews or sautéed to accompany steak.

You can remove the mushroom stem by cutting it with a knife or scissors right where it joins the cap, but this method will always leave a little bit of stem. I prefer to grasp the stem firmly and twist it in one swift motion while holding the cap in my other hand. This leaves a little depression in the middle of the cap.

USING PORTOBELLO MUSHROOMS

The whole cap offers the most possibilities for eating satisfaction—as pizzas, grilled mushrooms, and melts. Smaller caps (2–3 inches in diameter) don't really have to be prebaked, but as the cap becomes larger, it gets thicker and meatier as well. These larger caps need 3–6 minutes in an oven (or a minute or so in the microwave) so that the mushroom will be thoroughly cooked in the finished dish. However, it is okay for a portion of the cap to remain raw—in some cases, it is even desirable (e.g., when served as an hors d'oeuvre). The recipes in this book were tested using the caps available in 6-ounce packages in the grocery store—for the most part, the smaller caps. If you use really large caps (5–7 inches in diameter), you should increase the prebaking times.

Sliced mushrooms are usually ¼–½ inch thick, because they lose volume as they cook. Remember that mushrooms are nearly 90 percent water! Thin slices can yield gray, mushy, indistinct cooked pieces—something to be avoided in most cases. If you have purchased sliced mushrooms to make these recipes, the slices are usually kept whole, but there are a few recipes in which they are cut in half or into chunks. Portobellos should be sliced thinner than ¼ inch only when they are to be used raw, in salads.

Chunked portobellos can be cooked in several ways. If you have purchased sliced portobellos, cut them twice across the slices to make smaller bits. But you can make chunks or wedges from the very largest mushrooms by cutting pieces from them like slices from a pie, or by cutting them in half, then in half again, until you get a size you want. This is a good way to cut portobellos for pickling.

Stems are usually partially hollow and must be cut fairly thick or they will fall apart while you slice them. Cut the stem lengthwise for grilling.

Compared to other mushrooms, portobellos are meaty. That doesn't mean they are really anything like meat, no matter how much we would like them to be. But they are a substantial mouthful, and for the person looking for gustatory satisfaction without the fat and calories, portobellos could be the answer. Cooking them to maximize their meaty character and flavor is the point of this book. There are a few things to know before you get started.

First, like all mushrooms, portobellos are composed mostly of water, so, unlike meat, they really do lose considerable volume during cooking. The great thing about portobellos is that there's still plenty of mushroom left.

That water, and the fast rate at which it flees the mushroom during cooking, has certain implications for cooking. Portobellos must be "sweated" ahead of time for many uses or else they will yield the liquid in an unwanted way. For example, in the recipe for Spicy and Quick Portobello Lasagne (see page 62), the moisture from the mushrooms during baking would make the surrounding tomato sauce too thin. On the other hand, there are dishes like the Provence-Style Portobello Ragout (see page 69), in which the mushroom liquid becomes part of the sauce. You'll get the hang of it after doing some of the recipes in this book.

Second, except for very fresh portobellos (a week or less old), the mushrooms, especially the slices, become muddy gray if cooked by themselves. Darker sauces, using soy sauce, are a way of minimizing this problem. The simplest way, however, is to use only very fresh mushrooms when the portobellos are going to be front and center in a dish.

Third, the flavor of portobellos is full, rich, and earthy, but more delicate than you might think. Acids tend to diminish mushroom flavor, so use them with caution—avoid citrus, vinegar, or wine except in dishes where acidity is a counterpoint to the earthiness of the mushroom. Conversely, some ingredients emphasize the earthy flavor. Soy sauce is one of those ingredients. In fact, my favorite seasoning combination is salt, soy sauce, and a touch of sugar to maximize flavor. Plain salt is very good as well, especially in a simple dish like Basic Grilled Portobellos (see page 21). Another favorable ingredient, especially in whole-cap preparations, is cheese, including Gorgonzola, blue, and Stilton. This should come as no surprise, since the flavors of these cheeses come from the molds infecting them and mold is a fungus, just like a mushroom.

Portobellos often act like sponges for other flavors that come in contact with them. That's why overmarinating them in a vinegar-based liquid is so damaging. There is a recipe for the proper way to marinate portobellos on page 24. Also, if you use strong "painting sauces" like those described on page 67, be careful that you don't overdo it. Portobellos can be a wonderful canvas for other flavors, but keep the mushroom flavor at least as important as the other flavors.

Hot sauces go very well with portobellos. The Roasted Vegetable Portobello Pizza (see page 76) is also a good example of how heat and mushrooms coexist in a delirious riot of flavors.

Portobello
Basics

Basic Braised Portobellos with Herbs

This may be the simplest and quickest method for preparing portobellos as a side dish or a garnish for meat or fish. Older portobello caps work well in this recipe, but reduce the cooking time by about 1 minute.

1 tablespoon vegetable oil

1 6-ounce package sliced portobello caps

Salt

1 tablespoon chopped fresh herbs, such as oregano, thyme, or basil,

or a combination, or ¼ teaspoon dried herbs

Pour the oil into a 9-inch sauté pan and place over high heat for 30 seconds, then lower the heat to medium. Add the sliced mushrooms and sprinkle lightly with salt. Add 2 tablespoons of water to the pan and cover with a lid. Let simmer, covered, for 3 minutes.

Remove the lid (the mushrooms should have given up more liquid); the liquid should be at a vigorous boil. Add the herbs, stir, replace the lid, and simmer for another 2 minutes, until the flavors meld. Remove the lid and serve as a side dish. **Serves 2**

All-Purpose Pickled Portobellos

Pickling recipes can be tricky. We have tried hundreds in our restaurant over the years and find this one the best. It was included in my first book, *Joe's Book of Mushroom Cookery*, as well as in *A Cook's Book of Mushrooms,* and is repeated here because it is not easy to arrive at the essential balance required for a good marinade. Remember to blanch the portobellos before adding to the marinade. Tiny button mushrooms are also excellent when pickled. Refrigerated, these pickled mushrooms will keep for several days before they become limp. They are best if used right away.

I pound portobellos, cut into chunks

$1/2$ cup white wine vinegar

$1/4$ cup sugar

I tablespoon kosher salt

I tablespoon pickling spices

(or any combination of fresh or dried herbs,

using $1/2$ cup packed herbs if using fresh)

Place the portobello chunks in a deep saucepan and add $1/4$ cup of water. Bring the water to a boil and then cover the pan and turn the heat to medium. Blanch for 10 minutes, strain the mushrooms from the liquid, and let cool.

In a medium saucepan, combine the vinegar, sugar, and salt with I cup water and bring to a boil, stirring to dissolve the sugar and salt. Simmer for 5 minutes. Add the spices or herbs and remove from the heat. Let steep off the heat for a few minutes before adding the cooled mushrooms.

Makes 3 cups marinated mushrooms

basic grilled portobello

[or roasted]

Perhaps the most popular method of cooking portobellos is grilling. A summer feast outdoors is richly enhanced by this impressive and flavorful mushroom. The two most popular methods of grilling portobellos are as whole caps or skewered chunks, usually in combination with other vegetables, chicken, or fish. I have included a couple of recipes for grilling whole caps, in order to capitalize on the wonderful size and meatiness of the portobello. (You don't need to have summer weather to use these recipes. All of them can be prepared in a preheated 350° F. oven. Five minutes is all it takes for caps 2-3 inches in diameter. For larger caps, add a minute for each extra inch of diameter.)

But first, a few tips about roasting or grilling portobellos. It is possible to simply throw a large cap in the oven or over a grill, and it will cook without burning because of its high moisture content. However, you will end up with a wrinkled mushroom that will be dry, even chewy. This is because as the mushroom cooks, it gives up moisture. The flesh beneath the cap has more moisture than the cap itself, so it will lose moisture faster than the cap, causing it to shrink at a faster rate. Hence, the cap will wrinkle as the flesh beneath it shrinks and pulls the cap "skin" together.

To avoid wrinkling, brush the mushroom generously, top and bottom, with vegetable oil before grilling or roasting. The mushrooms will develop an attractive medium brown color as they cook and will remain moist.

In addition to coating the caps with oil, scoring the cap with a knife will help the mushroom retain its shape while cooking. An added benefit of scoring is that any ingredient you use to coat the caps will penetrate further into the cap and thus add flavor. For a typical 3-inch-wide cap, lightly and carefully score 3-4 incisions into the cap, barely breaking the flesh. Then score again 3-4 times at right angles to the first cuts. A few more scores are necessary for very large caps. But scoring alone does not retard wrinkles in the cap.

Portobello stems can be grilled as well, whole or sliced in half lengthwise. They take a little longer to cook than the caps.

Basic Grilled Portobellos

The flavor of portobellos is delicate, so they work very well as canvases for other flavorful ingredients. I know of no better addition than plain salt to bring out the natural flavor of the mushroom. A little soy sauce also helps.

4 portobello caps, 3-4 inches in diameter

Salt

Vegetable oil

Soy sauce

Have a grill preheated and ready, or preheat the oven to 350°F.

Lightly salt the underside of the caps. Then generously brush oil all over the caps, top and bottom. Sprinkle a little more salt on the underside. Brush a very little soy sauce over the underside of the cap. Turn the cap over and score, making very shallow incisions 3-4 times, then score again at right angles.

Place the caps on the grill or oven rack and cook for 2-3 minutes on each side. The caps will turn a medium brown. Remove and serve. **Serves 4**

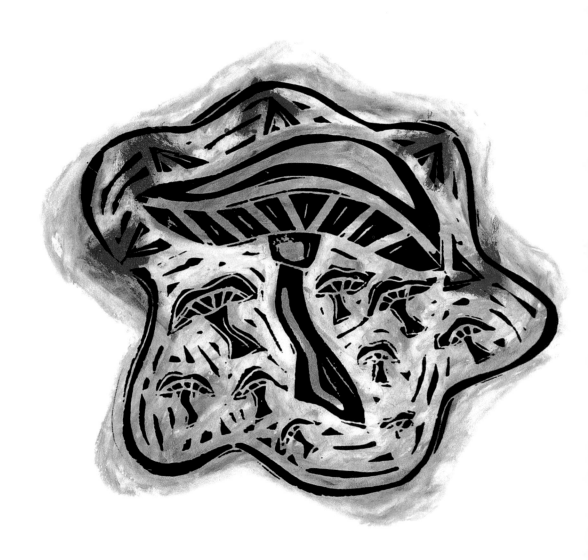

portobello "truffles"

Truffles cost more than $400 a pound these days, so they are not for every-day sprinkling over pasta. Many restaurants use shavings of truffles over dishes to impress you and jack up the price of whatever is underneath. Now you can do the same thing at home for a fraction of the price. Here's how.

Remove the stem of a portobello. (Younger, fresh portobellos are easier to work with, but the older caps will have a darker, more truffle-like color.) Place the cap on a plate with the gill side up. With a paring knife, cut the portobello in half and begin to scrape the gills away from the cap where they meet. You will notice that the gills look like small, rectangular chopped truffles as they drop onto the plate. Repeat with the other mushroom half. Sprinkle the "truffles" onto chicken, pasta, or risotto.

Marinated Grilled Portobellos

This recipe is a favorite of those who like marinated mushrooms. Remember, however, that portobellos act like sponges, so marinate the mushrooms for only a short period of time, or the resulting dish will be very vinegary and unpleasant. If you don't have a grill, bake the portobellos in a 350° F. oven for 5-7 minutes.

4 large portobello caps, 4-6 inches in diameter

I cup good-quality olive oil

I cup red or white wine vinegar

2 tablespoons soy sauce

I tablespoon sugar

I tablespoon dried herbs,

or ¹/₂ cup finely chopped fresh herbs.

Cut the stems from the caps of the mushrooms. Slice each stem lengthwise.

Combine the rest of the ingredients and blend well with a whisk for a minute or two. Let the marinade sit for I hour until the herbs soften.

Prepare a grill.

Place the mushrooms in a shallow dish or pan and pour the marinade over the mushrooms. Let the mushrooms marinate for 10 minutes, turning occasionally to ensure uniform coating.

Remove the mushrooms from the marinade and place on the hot grill. Grill on each side for 2-3 minutes. Remove from the grill, slice, and serve immediately. **Serves 4**

Portobello Duxelles

Duxelles is a mushroom paste that has been cooked down to release most of the liquid, a reduction of mushrooms to a concentrated form. My first book contained more than twenty variations on this basic recipes. Duxelles can be combined with fresh herbs, smoked salmon, chopped oysters, and many other strong-flavored ingredients to produce a great canapé topping or a wonderful coating for fish or meat. Frozen, duxelles can be kept for months, and I recommend that you prepare this in a large quantity so that you can pull from your freezer as needed.

The classic recipe uses champignon de Paris, or as we know them, button mushrooms, but portobellos are equally good—especially the stems, which make a more attractive and firm duxelles. Older caps are also good candidates for duxelles. You should chop the mushrooms by hand, rather than in a food processor. Duxelles should have some texture, which comes only from reducing finely cut, rather than mashed, mushrooms. It's good exercise.

3 tablespoons melted butter

2/3 cup chopped onion

2 cups finely chopped portobellos, about 8 ounces

1/4 teaspoon salt

1/4 teaspoon sugar

1/2 teaspoon soy sauce

Place the butter in a medium sauté pan over medium heat. Sauté the onion until just translucent, about 3 minutes. Add the mushrooms, salt, sugar, and soy sauce and stir slowly. The mushrooms will begin to give off liquid. Continue to stir the mushrooms until all the liquid has evaporated and the mixture resembles a semidry paste, 8-12 minutes. Remove from the heat and let cool. Store in the refrigerator or freezer. **Makes I cup**

Soups
and
Salads

Cream of Portobello Soup

Cream of Portobello Soup is a perennial favorite. The trick to making a good one is to use the juices from the mushroom, which provide maximum flavor. It is also important to use fresh, young mushrooms or mushroom stems, because the gills of older mushrooms tend to color the soup an unappetizing gray. If your mushrooms have very dark gills, scrape them off and sprinkle them over the soup.

5 tablespoons melted butter

3 tablespoons flour

3/4 cup chopped onion

1 6-ounce package portobello caps, stems, or slices, cut into 1-inch chunks

Salt

2 cups milk

2 cups heavy cream

1/4 teaspoon freshly ground black pepper

1/4 teaspoon dried thyme

2 tablespoons Marsala or sweet sherry

2 ounces Roquefort or blue cheese (optional)

Heat 3 tablespoons of the butter in a small saucepan over medium heat. Add the flour and stir constantly until a paste (roux) forms. Continue to stir and cook for another minute, until the flour is cooked. Remove from the heat and set aside.

Place the remaining 2 tablespoons of butter in a medium saucepan over medium heat. Add the onion and sauté until golden, about 2 minutes. Add 2 tablespoons of water to the pan and then add the mushrooms. Salt lightly, reduce the heat, and cover. Let the pan sit over the heat for about 10 minutes. Remove the lid and add the milk, cream, pepper, and thyme. Increase the heat and bring almost to a boil—when bubbles form around the edge of the pan. Stirring, add all of the butter-flour mixture to the milk. Add the Marsala or sherry and stir with a whisk over medium heat until the soup thickens, 3-4 minutes. Adjust for salt. Ladle the soup into bowls and sprinkle a little of the cheese over the top, if desired. Serve immediately. **Serves 4**

portobello crudités

Portobellos are great as one of the vegetables served raw on a plate of crudités. You can use the packaged sliced caps or whole caps. Remember, however, to keep the package covered or the caps whole until just before you are ready to use them, or else exposure to air will oxidize the mushrooms and they will begin to discolor. There are many dips you can use, but a simple blue cheese dressing is one of my favorites.

Another good dip is a dressing of fresh herbs. To make one, add ½ cup tightly packed herbs or watercress to a blender along with 1 tablespoon white wine vinegar and ¼ cup water. Blend to a puree. In a medium bowl, combine ⅔ cup mayonnaise with the herb puree and blend well. Refrigerate for at least 1 hour before using.

Portobello and Lemongrass Soup

Starting with this basic recipe, you can create an infinite variety of soups. If you want a vegetarian version, use vegetable stock or plain water instead of chicken stock. Adjust for salt when you finish the soup. This recipe also makes a great won-ton soup, especially with won tons filled with Portobello Duxelles (see page 25).

Older portobellos are okay for this soup, but their developed gills will make it very dark. It's best to remove the gills.

4 cups seasoned and lightly salted chicken stock,
or 4 cups Portobello Consommé (see page 36)
1 stalk lemongrass, finely chopped
(you can make a good soup by substituting
1 teaspoon lemon juice, but it will not have the same subtle character)
1 bunch scallions, white part thinly sliced,
green stalks left whole
1 6-ounce package sliced portobello caps, cut in half
1 cup cooked noodles for soup, well rinsed and drained
Cilantro sprigs, for garnish

Place the chicken stock in a medium saucepan. Add the lemongrass and the green scallion stalks. Bring to a boil, stir, then reduce the heat, and simmer for 10 minutes over very low heat. (This part can be done well ahead of time. You can even cool to room temperature, refrigerate, and use the next day.)

In another saucepan of the same size, add the mushrooms and white part of the scallions. Strain the broth over the mushrooms, discarding the lemongrass and green scallions. Cover the saucepan and bring the soup to a boil. Reduce the heat to low and simmer for 5 minutes. Add the noodles, or any other vegetables you would like (see Note) and simmer for another 5-7 minutes, until they are tender. Serve in individual bowls and garnish with large sprigs of cilantro. **Serves 4**

Note: There are many vegetables you could add to this soup. Just be sure that they are sliced thin enough to get tender in the 5 minutes they have to cook in the soup. Some of my favorites are Chinese (napa) cabbage and bok choy. Or use thinly sliced barbecued pork or duck (available in Chinese grocery stores).

Seasonal Greens with Shaved Portobellos

Any seasonal greens can be used for this recipe, as well as romaine, Boston, or red leaf lettuce. I prefer strongly flavored greens like arugula and watercress mixed with oak leaf lettuce. The Pickled Portobellos give the salad an extra tang. It's a good idea to make the dressing ahead of time to let the flavors mingle before using.

For the dressing

1/2 cup mayonnaise

1 tablespoon dry sherry

1 tablespoon Dijon mustard

1 teaspoon dried dill

1 teaspoon fresh lemon juice

For the salad

3 ounces whole portobello caps

6-8 cups mixed salad greens

1/4 cup chopped walnuts

1/2 cup All-Purpose Pickled Portobellos (page 17; optional)

Freshly ground black pepper

Make the dressing. Combine the mayonnaise, sherry, mustard, dill, and lemon juice in a blender and blend until smooth, about 30 seconds.

Slice the mushrooms as thin as possible and set aside. Place the cleaned salad greens in a large bowl. Toss the greens with the walnuts (and the pickled mushrooms, if using) and the dressing until well blended. Then toss gently with the sliced portobellos. Season with freshly ground pepper and serve immediately. **Serves 4**

Portobello Consommé or Light Stock

This stock is delicious in vegetarian soups and other dishes that call for chicken or veal stock.

4 cups water

2 6-ounce packages portobellos, chopped

2 tablespoons soy sauce

1 teaspoon salt

¹/₂ teaspoon sugar

Place the portobellos and 4 cups of water in a large saucepan with a tight-fitting lid. Bring to a boil over medium heat. Turn down the heat to low, cover, and simmer for 20 minutes.

Strain the liquid into a smaller saucepan and add the soy sauce, salt, and sugar. Place over medium heat and bring to a gentle simmer. Remove from the heat and let cool to room temperature. Store in the refrigerator or freeze for up to 6 months. **Makes 4 cups**

Portobello Salad with Balsamic Vinegar

Roasted red peppers are now available in most specialty stores. If they are not marinated, you can marinate your own roasted peppers in the marinade used for the Marinated Grilled Portobellos (see page 24).

Start with whole portobello caps for this salad, because you need thinner slices than those found in packages. Balsamic vinegar is generally available in specialty stores; buy the best you can afford. The very old ones are sweet with an acid edge perfect for this dish—although most good commercial brands will do. Do not substitute regular wine vinegar.

**I very large or 2 medium fresh tomatoes, sliced thin into about
as many pieces as you have of mozzarella**

2 balls fresh mozzarella cheese, cut into $1/2$-inch-thick rounds

$1/3$ cup extra-virgin olive oil

$1/3$ cup balsamic vinegar

2 whole portobello caps, 3-4 inches in diameter, thinly sliced

2 whole marinated roasted peppers, sliced into I-inch-wide pieces

2 tablespoons finely chopped fresh basil

Alternate the slices of tomato and mozzarella on 4 plates. Blend together the oil and balsamic vinegar and sprinkle half of it over the tomatoes and cheese. Then place the slices of mushrooms and peppers crossed over one another on top of the tomato and cheese, and sprinkle with the rest of the dressing. Finally, sprinkle the basil over top of the entire salad and serve. **Serves 4**

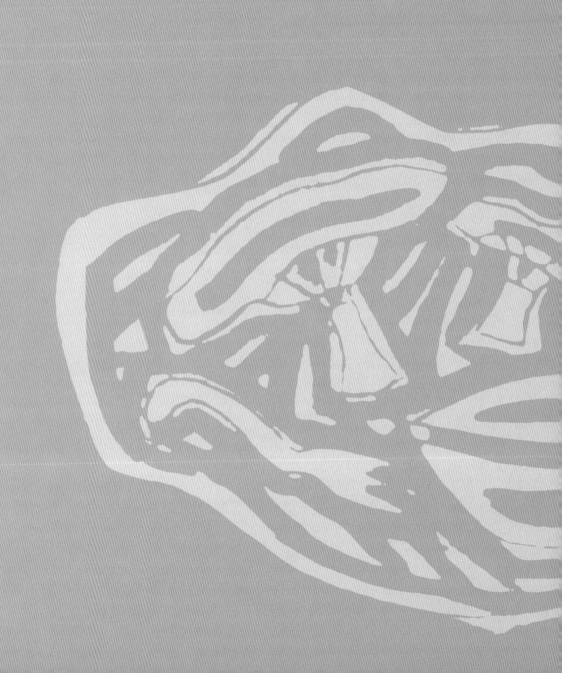

Main Course
Mushrooms

Stuffed Portobello en Croute

Stuffed portobellos encased in pastry are a wonderful preparation and I think this is the best way to make them. You can prepare this recipe with no stuffing at all, simply by "painting" the portobellos with the hoisin or oyster sauce. If you don't have hoisin sauce, paint the portobello cap with a little soy sauce in which some sugar has been dissolved.

1 whole portobello cap, 3-4 inches in diameter

Hoisin sauce

1 4 x 4-inch piece puff pastry (all-butter has the best flavor)

2 ounces Roquefort or other crumbly blue cheese

1/2 cup cooked chopped spinach

1 tablespoon thinly sliced scallion

1 egg, beaten

Preheat the oven to 425°F.

Paint the underside of the portobello cap with hoisin sauce. Roll out the puff pastry with a rolling pin to about 6 x 6 inches.

Crumble the cheese in the middle of the puff pastry. Cover the cheese with the portobello cap, gill side facing up. Cover the gills with the spinach and scallion. Fold in the 4 corners of the puff pastry so they overlap to enclose the whole cap and stuffing. Turn the cap over, score lightly with a knife in a decorative pattern, and brush on some of the beaten egg. Bake for 6-8 minutes, or until the crust is golden brown. Serve immediately. **Makes 1 stuffed cap**

Steak Smothered with Portobellos and Cheese

"**Q**uintessential" is the only term that can describe this combination. Rich, earthy mushrooms paired with the intense character of Roquefort and the essential goodness of American beef make this recipe an American classic. Choose the best marbled steaks you can find. I have written this recipe using a grill, but it can be prepared in the oven as well.

4 sirloin steaks, 8-10 ounces each

Vegetable oil

2 large onions, thinly sliced

1 6-ounce package sliced portobello caps

Salt

8 ounces Roquefort, blue, or gorgonzola cheese,

crumbled with a fork

Prepare a charcoal grill with a cover.

Score each steak through the fat around the edges, about 2 inches apart.

Pour a little oil into a skillet over medium heat. Add the onions and mushrooms and sauté until they are well wilted, about 5 minutes. Salt lightly to taste.

Grill the steaks. When they are 2-3 minutes short of desired doneness, top with the onion-mushroom mixture. Sprinkle the cheese over. Cover the grill and continue to cook until the cheese is melted, about 2 minutes. **Serves 4**

Note: *If you don't want to wait until warm weather to make these steaks, sear the steaks in a skillet. For medium rare, cover the steaks with the mushroom-onion mixture and place in an oven preheated to 400°F. Roast for 6-10 minutes. If you prefer steaks well done, cook them longer in the skillet before placing them in the oven.*

Sole with Portobellos

Mushrooms and fish always make an intriguing combination, but there are several important things to keep in mind, especially with delicate fish such as sole. Since mushrooms have a natural earthy flavor, lighten that character a bit with a little lemon juice (but not too much!). This portobello topping can be used with virtually any kind of fish, including oily fish like bluefish or salmon.

2 tablespoons vegetable oil

$^1/_2$ medium onion, coarsely chopped

2 teaspoons fresh lemon or lime juice

1 tablespoon soy sauce

1 6-ounce package sliced portobello caps

Salt

1 tablespoon chopped fresh dill or other herbs,

or $^1/_4$ teaspoon dried

4 sole fillets, 4-6 ounces each

Pour the oil in a large skillet with a cover over medium heat. Add the onion and sauté for about 30 seconds. Add the lemon juice and soy sauce. Add the mushrooms and season them lightly with salt. Continue to sauté, stirring gently the whole time, until the mushrooms become limp and lose their chalk white appearance. When the mushrooms are very soft, in 10-12 minutes, add the herbs. Continue tostir for another minute or so.

Season the sole fillets with salt and place over in the skillet the mushroom mixture. Cover and place over medium heat. Cook for 5-7 minutes, until the fillets are just cooked. Serve covered with the portobellos. **Serves 4**

Crab Cakes with Portobellos and Warm Mustard Vinaigrette

This recipe, which uses duxelles, is from Harry Holden, my chef at Joe's Bistro 614. Fresh lump crabmeat is the best, but you can use any kind, including frozen or pasteurized.

For the crab cakes

1/2 cup fresh bread crumbs

1/2 cup Portobello Duxelles (page 25)
or duxelles made from white button mushrooms or cremini

1 teaspoon cayenne pepper

1 tablespoon fresh or 1 teaspoon dried dill

1 egg, beaten lightly

1/2 cup mayonnaise

1 pound crabmeat

For the mustard vinaigrette

1/4 cup red wine vinegar

1/2 cup extra-virgin olive oil

1 1/2 teaspoons salt

1 tablespoon sugar

1 teaspoon crushed black peppercorns

1/4 teaspoon minced garlic

1 1/2 tablespoons Dijon mustard

2 tablespoons melted butter

2 tablespoons vegetable oil

Stir together the bread crumbs, duxelles, cayenne, dill, egg, and mayonnaise. When the mixture is completely blended, carefully fold in the crabmeat, taking care that it does not break up. Refrigerate this mixture for at least 1 hour.

While the crab mixture is in the refrigerator, make the vinaigrette. Combine the vinegar, olive oil, salt, sugar, pepper, garlic, and mustard in a blender. Blend thoroughly, then set aside.

When the crab mixture is cold, form crab cakes by rolling a small (about 3-4 ounces) amount of the mixture between your palms gently to form a ball. Then gently flatten the ball into the shape of a cake. Repeat for the rest of the mixture. You should have about 8 cakes.

Place a medium saucepan over medium heat and pour in the butter and oil. When the oil begins to bubble vigorously, add the crab cakes, 4 at a time. Fry until the cakes begin to brown, about 5 minutes. Flip over the cakes and repeat on the other side. Repeat this procedure for the remaining cakes. Keep the finished crab cakes warm.

Heat the vinaigrette very gently over medium heat in a saucepan or in the microwave until it is just warm. Spread the sauce in an even amount over 4 plates. Place 2 crab cakes on each plate and serve.

Serves 4

Heidi's Huevos

A cross between *huevos rancheros* and Eggs Benedict, this succulent use of portobellos is a tribute to my wife, Heidi.

2 tablespoons butter

2 tablespoons vegetable oil

2 large onions, thinly sliced

1 serrano chile, finely chopped (optional)

2 6-ounce packages sliced portobello caps

5 garlic cloves, minced

Salt

1 cup hot or mild salsa

8 large eggs

4 English muffins, split in half and toasted

8 ounces Monterey Jack cheese, grated (2 cups)

Preheat the oven to 350°F. Place the butter and oil in a large sauté pan over medium heat. Add the onions and chile and sauté for 2 minutes. Add the mushrooms and sauté until the mushrooms just begin to get limp, about 1 minute. Add the garlic and continue to sauté most of the liquid has evaporated, about 5 minutes. Salt to taste and remove from the heat, but keep warm.

Heat the salsa in a small saucepan or microwave. Keep warm.

Grease an 8-cup muffin pan (preferably nonstick) with a little oil. Crack a whole egg into each depression. Place in the oven and bake until set (5-7 minutes). While the eggs are baking, sprinkle the cheese over each English muffin half. Place in the oven 3 minutes before the eggs are done.

Place 2 muffin halves with cheese on each serving plate. Evenly divide the mushroom mixture among the 8 muffins. Then place an egg on each muffin half and finally spoon the salsa evenly on top of the eggs. Serve immediately. **Serves 4**

Shrimp Teriyaki Kabobs with Portobellos

This quick and satisfying summer grilled dish is the essence of simplicity. You can use any size shrimp, in any quantity. The marinade is a sweet and sour version of a teriyaki. It can be enhanced very easily with a little heat by adding the hot sauce of your choice or about $1/2$ teaspoon of minced jalapeño to the marinade itself. You can also use this recipe with chicken, pork, or beef.

8 ounces medium shrimp, peeled and deveined

1 medium onion, cut into chunks no thicker than 3 layers

1 bell pepper—green, red, or yellow—cut into chunks

1 6-ounce package sliced or whole portobello caps,
brushed with oil, then cut into 1-inch chunks

$1/4$ cup soy sauce

$1/4$ cup dry sherry

Juice of 1 lemon

2 tablespoons sugar

$1/4$ teaspoon Asian roasted sesame oil

1 tablespoon cornstarch mixed with $1/3$ cup cold water

Prepare a grill.

Alternate pieces of shrimp, onion, pepper, and mushroom on 4 skewers. Combine the soy sauce, sherry, lemon juice, sugar, and sesame oil. Stir well to dissolve the sugar.

Place the skewers in a shallow dish and pour over the marinade. Let stand in the marinade for 10 minutes, basting frequently. Drain, reserving the marinade. Pour the marinade into a small saucepan and bring to a low boil. Thicken with a little cornstarch mixture until the sauce coats a spoon. You may not need to use all of it. Remove from the heat.

Grill the skewers until the shrimp are done and the mushrooms have begun to wrinkle, 3 minutes per side over a normal fire.

Remove the shrimp and vegetables from the skewers and spoon a little of the thickened sauce over them. Serve immediately. **Serves 4**

Note: You can also make this dish in the oven. Preheat the oven to 350°F. Place the skewers on an oven rack fitted over a pan and bake for 6-7 minutes.

Variation: Use chunks of tomato and pineapple on the skewers for a Hawaiian touch.

Portobello Tempura with Beer Batter

Any part of the mushroom can be used in this dish, but it is a great way to use up portobello stems. This is a quick and easy snack for which you can use any dipping sauce or salad dressing. I think the best dipping sauces for this dish are honey-mustard sauce, tartar sauce, or blue cheese dressing. Any creamy salad dressing works well. If you like spicy flavors, as I do, try any of the chili sauces in Asian food markets.

4 cups vegetable oil, for frying

12 ounces beer

2 egg yolks

I teaspoon salt

3 cups flour, plus more for dredging

I 6-ounce package sliced portobello caps,
or stems sliced in half lengthwise

Dipping sauce, or juice of lime or lemon

Pour the oil into a sturdy 4-quart saucepan or skillet over medium heat. Use a thermometer to measure when the oil reaches 340°F.

While the oil is heating, in a bowl combine the beer, egg yolks, and salt. Stir well, then add the flour all at once and mix lightly; do not whip or worry about mixing until smooth leave the batter a little lumpy.

Dredge the mushroom pieces in some flour, then cover completely with the batter. When the oil is between 340 and 350°F., add 4-6 mushroom pieces. Fry until light golden, about I 1/2 minutes, then lift out and transfer to a plate lined with a paper towel. Repeat until all the mushrooms are fried. Serve immediately, with dipping sauce or lemon or lime juice. **Serves 4**

Spaghetti with Portobellos and Kielbasa

You can use any kind of pasta for this dish, except angelhair, which is too fine for the sauce to cling to. Young, fresh portobellos are best, but even so, the gills should be scraped away. You can make this dish without scraping off the gills, but the sauce may look muddy. The scrapings look very attractive, however, sprinkled over the top of the finished dish.

1 6-ounce package sliced portobello caps

12-16 ounces spaghetti

4 tablespoons vegetable oil

1/2 small onion, diced

4 garlic cloves, finely diced

4 ounces kielbasa (Polish sausage), cut into matchstick pieces

3/4 cup heavy cream

Salt

Scrape the gills from the mushroom slices and save. Cut each slice in half.

Bring a large pot of lightly salted water to a boil. Add the spaghetti and cook until it is al dente, 8-10 minutes. Drain.

While the pasta is cooking, place the oil in a large skillet over medium heat. Add the onion and garlic, and sauté for about 1 minute. Add the mushrooms and sausage and continue to sauté stirring constantly. The mushrooms will begin to give off liquid, but it will evaporate quickly. When the mushrooms are limp and the liquid has evaporated, about 6 minutes, add the cream. Turn the heat to low and simmer until the sauce begins to thicken. Salt to taste and toss the sauce with the spaghetti. Sprinkle the scraped gills over the spaghetti and serve immediately. **Serves 4**

Portobello Pot Pie with a Crumb Crust

You don't need a pastry crust for this pot pie, just some bread crumbs. It's best to use flat, wide egg noodles, but you can use fettuccini if you wish.

8 ounces flat, wide egg noodles or fettucini

1 tablespoon extra-virgin olive oil

1/2 cup chopped onion

1 6-ounce package sliced portobello caps

1 teaspoon salt

1 teaspoon sugar

1 tablespoon soy sauce

1/2 teaspoon dried savory

2 teaspoons cornstarch mixed with 1/4 cup cold water

2 cups dried bread crumbs

1/2 cup grated Parmesan cheese

1 tablespoon melted butter

Preheat the oven to 450°F. Fill a large pot half full of water. Salt the water, bring to a boil, and add the noodles. Cook until done, about 10 minutes. Drain and mix with a little oil.

While the noodles are cooking, place the olive oil in a large skillet over medium heat. Add the onion and sauté until slightly browned, 2-3 minutes. Add 1/2 cup water and the mushrooms, cover, and simmer for 10-12 minutes, until the mushrooms have given off a considerable amount of liquid.

Add the salt, soy sauce, and savory, and stir. Simmer for another 5 minutes. Add the cornstarch mixture and stir until thickened. Combine with the noodles and mix well.

Place the mushroom mixture in a shallow baking dish, cover evenly with the crumbs, and top with the cheese. Drizzle with butter and place in the oven for 5 minutes before serving. **Serves 4**

Portobello Omelet

This is a spicy version of a simple mushroom omelet. The large pieces of mushroom make it heartier, too. The mushrooms can be mixed into the eggs, but I prefer to use them as a stuffing. For a frittata, mix the eggs with the mushroom mixture and scramble.

2 tablespoons butter

1/2 cup thinly sliced onion

1/3 cup very thinly sliced red bell pepper

1 teaspoon finely minced hot chile pepper,

such as serrano or jalapeño

3 ounces sliced portobellos or 1 medium cap, sliced

1/4 teaspoon dried savory (optional)

Salt

3 eggs

Vegetable oil

1/3 cup grated sharp Cheddar cheese

Melt the butter in a medium skillet and add the onion, bell pepper, and chile. Sauté for 1 minute. Add the mushrooms and continue to sauté until the mushrooms have become limp and any liquid has evaporated, 6-8 minutes. Add the savory, stir, and add salt to taste—the flavor should be quite assertive. Keep warm.

Beat the eggs. Place a large nonstick skillet over low heat, add just a bit of oil, and pour in the eggs. Cook until the eggs begin to set, about 1 minute. Sprinkle the cheese over the eggs, cover with the mushroom mixture, and flip half the omelet over the other half. Remove from the heat and serve immediately. **Serves 1-2**

Portobello-Vegetable Stir-Fry

The art of stir-frying is in the cutting. Make sure the vegetables approximate each other in size and shape, so they can cook in the same amount of time. This dish is good served over sticky rice or noodles flavored with a little sesame oil. Older caps are best because they have the most intense flavor, but younger caps are fine, too. You can add pieces of chicken, pork, or beef along with the vegetables. Chinese markets have great prepared meats such as Chinese sausage, barbecued pork, and duck, which can also be used.

2 tablespoons peanut oil

2 bunches scallions, white part only, sliced into 1-inch pieces

2 garlic cloves, minced

5 napa cabbage leaves, leafy part removed,

ribs cut into 2-inch pieces

4 large bok choy leaves, leafy part removed,

ribs cut into 2-inch pieces

1 6-ounce package sliced portobello caps,

cut into 2-inch chunks; or small whole caps, cut into wedges

3 tablespoons Chinese oyster sauce

1 tablespoon Hoisin sauce

1 tablespoon Chinese chili sauce

Place the oil in a wok over high heat when I the oil just begins to smoke, add the scallions, garlic, napa cabbage, bok choy, and mushrooms and stir-fry vigorously for 4-5 minutes, until the mushrooms lose some volume and the other vegetables begin to become translucent. Add the oyster, hoisin, and Chinese chili sauces and continue to stir-fry until the sauce is well blended with the vegetables. Remove from the heat and serve immediately. **Serves 4**

Arizona Bow-Tie Pasta with Portobellos

This variation on pasta with tomato sauce was inspired by the spicy cuisine of the American Southwest.

12-16 ounces bow-tie pasta

1 tablespoon vegetable oil

1 small onion, chopped

1 serrano chile, finely chopped

(or 2-or-3 if you really like it hot)

2 6-ounce packages sliced portobello caps or 12 ounces stems

2 teaspoons salt

1 tablespoon finely chopped fresh basil

1 tablespoon finely chopped fresh rosemary

3 tablespoons tomato paste

2 tablespoons barbecue sauce

Fill a large pot half full with water and add a little salt. Bring to a boil and add the pasta. Return to a simmer and let cook until the pasta is done, 7-8 minutes.

While the pasta is cooking, pour the oil into a large saucepan over medium heat. Sauté the onion for 1 minute. Add the chile and sauté for another minute. Add the mushrooms and sauté for 1 minute, or until a little liquid is drawn from the mushrooms. When you see the liquid forming at the bottom of the saucepan, cover with a tight-fitting lid, reduce the heat to low, and braise for 10 minutes.

Remove the lid and add the salt, basil, rosemary, tomato paste, and barbecue sauce. Stir and continue to simmer over low heat until the mixture begins to thicken. It should be slightly thick without being runny. If it does not thicken sufficiently, add a little more tomato paste. Place the pasta in a serving bowl and pour the sauce over it. Serve immediately. **Serves 4**

portobello tempura sandwich

[with Spicy Mayonnaise]

Place slices of Portobello Tempura (see page 50) on 4 slices of French bread.

Combine ½ cup of regular mayonnaise with 1 teaspoon of Tabasco and 2 tablespoons of hamburger relish. Spread 4 more slices of bread with the spicy mayonnaise and cover the tempura slices to make 4 sandwiches.

Angelhair Pasta with Portobellos, Leeks, and Balsamic Vinegar

This low-fat preparation truly satisfies.

10 ounces dried angelhair pasta

5 tablespoons extra-virgin olive oil

1 large leek or 2 bunches scallions,
cut into ¼-inch pieces including some of the green

4 garlic cloves, minced

1 6-ounce package sliced portobello caps

1 tablespoon balsamic vinegar

Salt

Pour the oil into a sauté pan and heat over medium heat for about 30 seconds. Sauté the leek for 2 minutes until softened. Add the garlic and sauté for another 30 seconds. Add the mushrooms and sauté, stirring frequently, until the mushrooms are wilted and the liquid they have given off has evaporated. Add the balsamic vinegar, stir well, and season with salt to taste.

Bring a large pot of lightly salted water to a boil and add the pasta, stirring to make sure the pasta is well separated. Boil 2-3 minutes, until done. Drain and transfer to a large bowl. **Serves 4**

Portobello and Bacon Quiche with Roquefort

You can make the quiche using Portobello Duxelles (see page 25) instead of the sautéed onion-mushroom mixture. Simply stir about ½ cup of duxelles into the custard mixture and pour into the crust.

2 tablespoons butter

I small onion, finely diced

I garlic clove, minced

I 6-ounce package sliced portobello caps

3 pieces bacon, cooked and crumbled

Salt

½ cup milk

½ cup heavy cream

2 eggs

¼ teaspoon dried savory (optional)

I prebaked 9-inch pie crust

3 ounces Roquefort cheese, crumbled (¾ cup)

3 ounces sharp Cheddar cheese, grated (¾ cup)

Preheat the oven to 450°F. Place the butter in a large skillet over medium heat. Sauté the onion and garlic for 30 seconds. Add the mushrooms and bacon, and continue to sauté until the mushrooms become very limp and any liquid is evaporated, 6-7 minutes. Salt to taste.

Combine the milk, cream, eggs, and savory. Spread the mushroom-bacon mixture evenly over the bottom of the crust. Then sprinkle the cheeses over the mixture. Cover with the egg mixture.

Bake for 10 minutes, then reduce the heat to 350°F. and bake for 20 minutes more. Check for doneness by piercing with a fork, which should come out clean. Let rest for 15 minutes, or cool to room temperature, refrigerate, then reheat for 7 minutes in a 350°F. oven before serving. **Serves 6**

Spicy and Quick Portobello Lasagne

The meaty goodness of portobellos is evident in this vegetarian lasagne. This dish is very good using older portobellos. The liquid they yield during cooking makes the sauce a very attractive dark red. The addition of hot chiles to the sauce also adds to the satisfying qualities of this dish. If you can't stand the heat, omit the chiles.

This dish can be prepared in advance, refrigerated, and heated later. In fact, it's better if the assembled dish has a day or two to sit in the refrigerator before baking. Add another 15 to 20 minutes to the baking time if you are going to heat it right from the refrigerator.

For a lower-calorie version, substitute any low-fat cheese or spaghetti sauce. And by all means, add sautéed ground beef or pork if you like a meaty lasagne.

8 ounces lasagne noodles (9 noodles)

2 6-ounce packages sliced portobellos

Salt

Dried oregano, to taste

1 jalapeño or 2 serrano chiles, minced

1 28-ounce jar tomato-based spaghetti sauce

(marinara, chunky vegetable, and so forth)

1 15-ounce container ricotta cheese

12 ounces shredded mozzarella or romano cheese (3 cups)

Preheat the oven to 350°F. Bring a large pot of lightly salted water to a boil. Add the lasagne noodles and cook for 12-to-15 minutes, until soft. You should be able to prepare everything else, except the baking, while the noodles are cooking.

Place the mushrooms in a large (6-8 quart) pot and add ¼ cup water. Lightly salt the mushrooms, turn the heat to high, and cover. When the liquid begins to boil (in about 1 minute), remove the lid, sprinkle a little oregano over the mushrooms, stir, and cover again. Turn the heat down to medium-low. After 6-8 minutes, the mushrooms will have given off much of their liquid and there will be about $1/2$ cup in the pot.

Gently lift the mushrooms out of the liquid and set aside. Add the chile to the pot. Turn the heat back to high, and evaporate most of the liquid until only a scant 2-3 tablespoons is left. Do not let the liquid residue burn. Add the tomato sauce and mix well. Turn off the heat.

Assemble the lasagne in a 13 x 9 x 2-inch baking dish. Place 3 noodles in the bottom of the dish. Spread one third of the ricotta and $1/2$ cup of the mozzarella over the noodles, then add one third of the mushrooms and one third of the sauce. Sprinkle a little oregano over the sauce. Repeat 2 more times. For the top layer, sprinkle on the rest of the mozzarella cheese. Cover the pan with aluminum foil, place in the oven, and bake for 20 minutes, or until heated through. Let the lasagne sit for about 15 minutes before serving to make it easier to cut. **Serves 6 to 8**

Garlic and Onion Risotto with Shaved Portobellos and Fragrant Oil

Raw portobellos have that almost crisp, chalky character of raw white button mushrooms, but that texture is lost in the cooking process. Shaved raw portobellos can add an intriguing flavor and texture to a dish. It is possible to shave a portobello cap with a peeler, but I find the best method is to cut the portobello as thin as possible with a sharp knife, which is easy because the raw mushroom is very firm. Shaved portobello, with its mild nutty flavor, is the treat of this dish. Its texture is a subtle counterpoint to the creamy consistency of the risotto.

Truffle oil is spectacular with this dish, but any flavored oil—such as rosemary or thyme oil—will do very well. Use vegetable stock (see page 36) or water if you want a vegetarian dish.

I 6-ounce package portobello caps or 2 whole portobellos with stems

6 tablespoons butter

4 large white onions, finely chopped

10 garlic cloves, minced

Salt

I cup arborio rice

5 cups chicken stock, vegetable stock, or water

I bunch scallions, green and white parts, thinly sliced

Truffle or flavored oil

If you are using mushroom caps, finely chop half of them. If you are using whole mushrooms, finely chop the stems. Reserve the remaining caps for shaving just before the risotto is served.

Place the butter in a large saucepan over medium heat. Add the onions and garlic and sauté for about I minute, until they are translucent. Add the mushrooms and sauté for another minute. Lightly salt to taste. The mixture will look a little mushy, because the mushrooms give off liquid. Add the rice and stir for 30 seconds. Add 1 cup of stock and stir until the liquid has been absorbed by the rice. Add another cup of stock and continue stirring. Continue adding stock in 1-cup amounts until most of the liquid has been absorbed, in 30-40 minutes. Taste the rice. It should be just slightly firm, but not raw in the middle. Cover and let stand off the heat for 10 minutes.

While the risotto is resting, cut the portobello caps into very thin slices using a very sharp knife, or shave them with a peeler.

Divide the risotto evenly among 4 bowls. Completely cover the risotto with shaved portobellos. Sprinkle the scallions over the mushrooms and drizzle about 2 teaspoons of truffle or flavored oil over each bowl just before serving. **Serves 4**

Note: Truffle oil can be found in specialty food stores. You can make our own herb oil as well. To 1 cup of extra-virgin olive oil add 1 ounce of coarsely chopped or small whole sprigs of fresh herbs, including the stems. Let the herbs sit in the oil for 1-2 weeks, shaking once a day. Strain the oil before using or leave the herbs in the oil. You can also make the oil using dried herbs, just use one third of the amount.

Grilled Portobellos Chinese Style

If you haven't already done so, you should become familiar with your local Asian grocery store. Grilled portobellos are extremely good with many standard Asian sauces. Unlike A-1 or Worcestershire sauce, which are vinegary, Chinese sauces, such as oyster sauce and black bean sauce, are very good to paint portobellos. Remember that the portobello flavor is delicate, and the flavor of mushrooms prepared in this fashion will be strong with the flavor of those sauces. Hoisin sauce is also very good, but it must be used sparingly because it is sweet.

This preparation can be a meal in itself, served with rice or noodles. It is also good as a side dish with steak or chicken.

**4 portobello caps,
about 3 inches in diameter**

Vegetable oil

**Chinese oyster sauce, chili,
or black bean sauce**

Brush the caps generously with the oil. Score the caps. Then brush the sauce over the top and on the underside of the mushrooms. Proceed as for Basic Grilled Portobellos (see page 21). **Serves 4**

Chicken with Portobellos, Potatoes, and Wine

This is a hearty, quick, and easy dish for a late winter's night. The sauce goes well with game birds, too.

Thighs and drumsticks of 2 chickens

4 large russet potatoes, cut in half crosswise

Vegetable oil

2 6-ounce packages sliced portobello caps, cut in half

1 cup dry red wine

1 tablespoon sugar

6 tablespoons Chinese oyster sauce

1 tablespoon chopped garlic

2 tablespoons dried herbs

$1/4$ cup cornstarch mixed with $1/2$ cup water

Preheat the oven to 400°F.

Lightly salt the chicken pieces, brush with oil, and lay on a large roasting rack. Coat the potato pieces well with oil and lay on rack with the chicken pieces. Place in the oven and cook until done, about 45 minutes. The potatoes should be soft and the chicken should yield a clear juice when pierced with a skewer.

Meanwhile, place the mushrooms in a medium saucepan over high heat. Add $1/4$ cup water, cover, and bring to a boil. Turn the heat down to medium and continue cooking for another 6 minutes.

Remove the mushrooms from the liquid. To the liquid in the saucepan add $1/2$ cup water, the wine, sugar, oyster sauce, garlic, and herbs. Simmer for 2 minutes over low heat, then thicken the sauce with the cornstarch mixture (do not overthicken!) and return the mushrooms to the sauce.

Arrange a thigh and drumstick along with 2 pieces of potato on each plate, cover with the mushroom sauce, and serve immediately. **Serves 4**

Quick Provence-Style Portobello Ragout

For a quick, one-skillet dish, this can't be beat. This method can be used for many different types of meat, whether fresh or cooked leftovers. Any number of vegetables can be used also, but the dish should have some brightly colored vegetables for aesthetic appeal. Caps are preferred because they tend to release more liquid than stems. If you use stems, simply add more water.

2 tablespoons extra-virgin olive oil

3 large garlic cloves, finely chopped

5 ounces yellow summer squash, sliced

1 medium red onion, cut into chunks

$\frac{1}{2}$ red bell pepper, cut into chunks

$\frac{1}{2}$ green or yellow bell pepper, cut into chunks

12 ounces leftover chicken (or beef, lamb, turkey)

Salt

1 6-ounce package sliced portobello caps, cut in half

2 tablespoons minced fresh herbs, such as thyme, marjoram, sage, oregano

2 tablespoons soy sauce

$\frac{1}{2}$ teaspoon sugar

2 teaspoons cornstarch dissolved in $\frac{1}{4}$ cup water

Place the oil in a large skillet over medium heat. Add the garlic, squash, onion, peppers, and chicken. Lightly salt the mixture and sauté over medium-high heat for 2 minutes.

Add the mushrooms and herbs along with $\frac{1}{2}$ cup water. Turn the heat to low, cover, and cook for 7 minutes. Remove the cover, add the soy souce and sugar, stir again, and thicken carefully with the cornstarch mixture. Serve immediately. **Serves 4**

Side Dishes and Snacks

Portobello "Cheesesteaks"

I was born in the cheesesteak capital of the world. No, not Philadelphia, which unjustly gets credit for the cheesesteak, but Reading, Pennsylvania, where the cheesesteak was born and where the best ones are still made today. You see, a real cheesesteak is not a dry affair topped with Cheez-whiz, or the way it's made in Philly. The real McCoy is always made with a spicy tomato sauce and always includes caramelized fried onions. Although the following recipe uses portobellos as a vegetarian substitute for the steak, go ahead and add grilled, thinly sliced steak to experience the real thing. Keep the mushrooms in there for a great experience and don't forget the sliced hot peppers.

Also, it is important to season the mushrooms well. The roll and sweet onions can dull the flavors of the mushrooms and sauce if they are not assertive enough.

1 6-ounce package sliced portobello caps

Salt

Vegetable oil

1/2 large onion, thinly sliced

1/2 teaspoon dried oregano

4 slices American, Romano, or mozzarella cheese

2 long sandwich buns (usually sold as hoagie buns, typically 6-8 inches long)

1/3 cup sliced cherry peppers or banana peppers

Place the mushrooms in a large saucepan and liberally sprinkle with salt. Add 1/4 cup water, turn the heat to medium, and cover. After 6 minutes the mushrooms will have released most of their liquid. Salt again so the mushroom flavor is very strong, and remove and place the mushrooms on a towel-lined plate.

Place about 2 tablespoons oil in an 8-inch sauté pan and add the onion. Fry the onion until very limp and browned, about 10 minutes. Turn down the heat to low, and season with a little salt and the oregano. Form the onion into a rectangular shape to approximate the shape of the buns into which they will go. Cover with the cheese. Cover the sauté pan and keep on the heat until the cheese melts. Remove the cover and cut the onion-cheese mixture down the middle so you have 2 thin, narrow halves. (By doing this, you make it easier to transfer the mixture onto the buns.)

Cut the buns almost in half lengthwise, making sure the "hinge" stays fully intact. Place half the onion-cheese mixture onto each bun with a spatula and add half the mushrooms. Cover with the warm sauce and finally add the hot peppers. **Makes 2 sandwiches**

Note: To make this a true cheesesteak, cook the meat while you fry the onions. Then blend the two together, form the mixture into a rectangular shape to approximate the rolls you are using, add and melt the cheese, and transfer to the buns. Cover with the sauce and add hot peppers.

portobellos with grilled steak

[on toasted french bread]

Grill a steak to your liking while preparing Basic Grilled Portobellos (see page 21). Brush 4 pieces of French bread with a little oil, and sprinkle with some minced garlic. Place the bread on the grill to toast. Put the toast on a plate and place a grilled portobello cap over it, then add the steak. Top the steak with a little sauce of your choice or a little soy sauce. The toast will soak up the delicious mushroom and steak juices.

Roasted Vegetable Portobello Pizza

This is a great way to use leftover grilled vegetables. If you don't have any on hand, follow the directions below for roasting.

1/2 cup white wine vinegar

1/4 cup sugar

I tablespoon kosher salt

4 portobello mushroom caps, 3-5 inches in diameter

2 tablespoons Chinese oyster sauce

2 bell peppers, preferably yellow or red, cut into quarters

4 jalapeño peppers, sliced in half, stems but not seeds removed

I bunch small scallions

4 1/2-inch-thick eggplant slices

4 ounces Mexican Chihuahua or other good melting cheese, such as
Monterey Jack, grated or sliced

Preheat the oven to 400°F. In a small saucepan, combine the vinegar, sugar, and salt and add 1 1/2 cups of water. Bring to a boil and stir to dissolve the salt and sugar. Remove from the heat and set aside.

Cut off of the portobello stems and reserve for another purpose. Paint the gill sides with oyster sauce and set aside.

Place the peppers, scallions, and eggplant in a baking dish and put in the oven. Roast for 10-15 minutes, until the peppers are pliable and have lost their firmness. Remove from the oven and place the vegetables in a bowl. Pour in the marinade, stir, and set aside for 15 minutes, stirring frequently.

Strain the vegetables from the marinade and distribute them evenly over the caps. Cover with the cheese and place in the oven for 7-8 minutes, or until the cheese is melted. Serve immediately.

Serves 4

Baked Potatoes with Portobello-Sour Cream Topping

A rich, zingy topping on a simple baked potato is always a treat. You can make the topping while the potato bakes. This dish is especially good if you use portobello stems.

4 baking potatoes

Vegetable oil

1 tablespoon butter

1 medium onion, coarsely chopped

1 6-ounce package portobello caps or stems,

cut into 1-inch chunks

Salt

2 teaspoons soy sauce

¼ teaspoon dried herbs, or 1 tablespoon chopped fresh herbs

⅓ cup sour cream

Preheat the oven to 450°F. Brush the potatoes with oil and place on the baking rack. Baked about 45 minutes. If the potatoes are a little firm on the inside when inserting a knife to test, let the potatoes rest for 5 minutes before serving.

While the potatoes are baking, place the butter in a large sauté pan. Add the onion and sauté for about 30 seconds over medium heat. Add the mushrooms, season lightly with salt, and sauté for 3 minutes, until the mushrooms become limp. Add the soy sauce and continue to sauté over medium-low heat until the mushrooms have released about 1 tablespoon of liquid. (Stems will release less.) Add the herbs and stir for another minute. Add the sour cream and stir well to blend with the mushrooms. Remove from the heat and keep warm until the potatoes are done.

Remove the potatoes from the oven, split in half, and pour one quarter of the mushroom topping in each. Serve immediately. **Serves 4**

Portobello "Pizza"

One of the most dramatic ways to take advantage of the size and meatiness of a portobello cap is to substitute it for a pizza crust. And it's much quicker and easier to make a Portobello Pizza than a regular one. Smaller caps, found in 6-ounce packages in grocery stores, are fine for making these mini-pizzas. If they measure 4 inches or less, you don't have to prebake them. Very large caps, however, need to be baked for about 5 minutes in a 350°F. or in a microwave at the highest setting for 1 minute oven before you proceed with the toppings. Use any of your favorite pizza toppings—pepperoni, sausage, onions, peppers, and so forth. (Most people prefer to eat this pizza with a knife and fork)

**1 6-ounce package portobello caps,
or 4 whole portobello caps**

A little oil, for brushing

1/2 cup tomato sauce

5 ounces mozzarella or any other good melting cheese

Preheat the oven to 350°F.

Wipe the caps clean of any dirt and brush lightly with oil. Place them on a baking dish, gill side up. Cover generously with the sauce, then top with the cheese. Place in the oven and bake for 6-8 minutes, or until the cheese is well melted. Serve immediately. (Most people prefer to eat this pizza with a knife and fork.) **Serves 4**

Open-Faced Portobello-Barbecue Melt

Ground beef or pork, or shredded meat of any kind, is ideal for this dish. I like to sauté hot peppers with the onions.

1 portobello cap

Vegetable oil

1/2 small onion, sliced

2-3 ounces ground beef (or pork, lamb, or shredded meat)

3 tablespoons barbecue sauce

Salt

1 slice mozzarella or Monterey Jack cheese

Preheat the oven to 350°F.

   Brush the cap with oil, place on an oven rack, and bake for 2 minutes. In 1 tablespoon oil, sauté the onion for 1 minute. Add the meat and sauté until the meat is browned and not showing any more red, 5-10 minutes. Stir in the barbecue sauce and season, if necessary. Remove the cap from the oven and cover with the meat mixture. Cover with the cheese and return to the oven until the cheese melts, about 1 minute. Serve immediately. **Serves 1**

Portobello Burgers

Yes, there is a reason portobellos are shaped like hamburger patties. Easy to prepare and very versatile, this recipe is just a starting point. You can garnish portobello burgers as you would your favorite hamburger. You can cook them on a grill, but the time may vary a little because caps cooking over direct heat need to be flipped once or twice to prevent scorching. Also, you need to use a grill with a cover in order to melt the cheese. (See also the recipe for Basic Grilled Portobellos, page 21).

You can also prepare regular hamburgers and simply place these Portobello Burgers on top.

4 portobello caps, 3-4 inches in diameter

Salt

1 tablespoon corn or peanut oil

4 slices American or Jack cheese

4 toasted hamburger buns

Cut off any residual stems from the caps so that the caps will lie flat. Lightly salt the gill side of the caps.

Place a 10-12 inch nonstick pan over high heat and add the oil. Before the oil starts smoking, add the caps, gill side down. Reduce the heat to medium and let the caps cook for 2 minutes.

Turn the caps and cook for another minute. Carefully place the cheese inside the caps and cover the pan with a lid (it does not have to be tight fitting) and cook for another minute, until the cheese is melted.

Transfer the caps to the buns and add any of your favorite toppings lettuce, slices of tomato and onion, and, of course, relish. Cover with the other half of the bun and serve. **Serves 4**

Variation: Chop the portobello stems you sliced from the caps and sauté them in a little oil with some sliced onions and minced garlic. When the onion mixture is well wilted and golden brown, remove from the pan and place on the top half of the bun. Then cook the caps and place them on top of the onion mixture. For a Pizzaburger, add a little warmed tomato sauce, flavored with oregano or basil.

Portobellos with Port

The sweet, rich taste of port with walnuts and Stilton cheese is a classic combination. This recipe is a nod to it, but you don't need the port to enjoy it. As an hors d'oeuvre by itself, it is quick and easy. Any good blue cheese can be used.

1 6-ounce package portobello caps

Vegetable oil

1/2 cup coarsely chopped walnuts

4 ounces blue cheese, crumbled (1 cup)

Preheat the oven to 350°F.

Wipe the caps clean and brush them with a little oil. Place in the oven on an oven rack and heat for 3 minutes. Remove from the oven and evenly fill the caps with the walnuts and then the cheese. Return to the oven until the cheese is melted, about 2 minutes.

Serve as an appetizer with knives and forks, or cut into quarters and pass as an hors d'oeuvre to be picked up by hand. **Serves 4**

Conversions

Weight equivalents

The metric weights given in this chart are not exact equivalents, but have been rounded up or down slightly to make measuring easier.

Avoirdupois	Metric
1/4 oz	7 g
1/2 oz	15 g
1 oz	30 g
2 oz	60 g
3 oz	90 g
4 oz	115 g
5 oz	150 g
6 oz	175 g
7 oz	200 g
8 oz (1/2 lb)	225 g
9 oz	250 g
10 oz	300 g
11 oz	325 g
12 oz	350 g
13 oz	375 g
14 oz	400 g
15 oz	425 g
16 oz (1 lb)	450 g
1 lb 2 oz	500 g
1 1/2 lb	750 g
2 lb	900 g
2 1/4 lb	1 kg
3 lb	1.4 kg
4 lb	1.8 kg
4 1/2 lb	2 kg

Volume equivalents

These are not exact equivalents for the American cups and spoons, but have been rounded up or down slightly to make measuring easier.

American	Metric	Imperial
1/4 t	1.25 ml	
1/2 t	2.5 ml	
1 t	5 ml	
1/2 T (1 1/2 t)	7.5 ml	
1 T (3 t)	15 ml	
1/4 cup (4 T)	60 ml	2 fl oz
1/3 cup (5 T)	75 ml	2 1/2 fl oz
1/2 cup (8 T)	125 ml	4 fl oz
2/3 cup (10 T)	150 ml	5 fl oz (1/4 pint)
3/4 cup (12 T)	175 ml	6 fl oz (1/3 pint)
1 cup (16 T)	250 ml	8 fl oz
1 1/4 cups	300 ml	10 fl oz (1/2 pint)
1 1/2 cups	350 ml	12 fl oz
1 pint (2 cups)	500 ml	16 fl oz
2 1/2 cups	625 ml	20 fl oz (1 pint)
1 quart (4 cups)	1 litre	1 3/4 pints

Oven Temperature equivalents

Oven	°F.	°C.	Gas Mark
very cool	250–275	130–140	1/2–1
cool	300	150	2
warm	325	170	3
moderate	350	180	4
moderately hot	375	190	5
	400	200	6
hot	425	220	7
very hot	450	230	8
	475	250	9

Butter

Some confusion may arise over the measuring of butter and other hard fats. In the United States, butter is generally sold in a one-pound package, which contains four equal "sticks." The wrapper on each stick is marked to show tablespoons, so the cook can cut the stick according to the quantity required. The equivalent weights are:

1 stick = 115 g/4 oz
1 T = 15 g/½ oz

Eggs

Unless otherwise noted, all recipes in this book use American large size eggs, which are equivalent to British standard-size eggs.

Flour

American all-purpose flour is milled from a mixture of hard and soft wheats, whereas British plain flour is made mainly from soft wheat. To achieve a near equivalent to American all-purpose flour, use half British plain flour and half strong bread flour.

Ingredients and Equipment Glossary

British English and American English are not always the same, particularly in the kitchen. The following ingredients and equipment used in this book are pretty much the same on both sides of the Atlantic, but have different names:

American	British
bell pepper	sweet pepper (capsicum)
broiler/to broil	grill/to grill
cornstarch	cornflour
eggplant	aubergine
heavy cream (37.6% fat)	double cream (35-40% fat)
peanut oil	groundnut oil
scallion	spring onion
skillet	frying pan

index

DESIGNED AND ILLUSTRATED BY ALEXANDRA MALDONADO

TYPEFACES IN THIS BOOK ARE CONTRIVANCE, BAUER BODONI AND HUMANIST

PRINTED BY TOPPAN PRINTING COMPANY, LTD.

TOKYO, JAPAN